we're
excited.
thank you
for being
here.

—Rumi

Black Author Brand Publishing
1601 Willow Lawn Dr Ste. 304
The Shops at Willow Lawn #1259
Richmond, VA 23230
www.blackauthorbrand.com

this
book
is for

me. and i know that sounds enormously self-serving, **but i needed to release these pieces for my journey in healing, expression, and freedom.** i pray you understand because this book is for you too, and i want you to do more than just read it. **my desire is that you will experience each piece deeply while reading, listening, imagining, and connecting it to your own life + feelings**. i hope that you hear me.

this. is our space. **welcome. to all the thinkers, feelers. welcome.** to all the extroverts, introverts, and 50:50 mixes, i'm so glad you're here. **promise me something.** that you'll take this book in slowly. **don't rush. there are things i don't want you to miss + feelings that i need you to feel.** i broke it up for you; **in thoughts + pieces. enjoy.**

+ means "and"

my brain moves fast
thoughts. come quick
right down the middle, evenly split
birthed left + right-brained, unapologetic
long story short, underneath this eclectic poetic
is a "die-hard" lover of math + aesthetic
a nerd with a deep appreciation for symbols + signs
i use them in my writing spaces to empty my mind
more efficiently + it really helps
capture ideas + feelings felt
so as you're reading words with plus signs
used in place of "and" sometimes
know that i captured my mind for you
in thoughts + pieces

love+
context

RUMI

love
followed
me
***

love followed me **in a box**
i was told to put myself in
and in that box, **we fought constantly**
cramped + uncomfortable
limited air supply; we suffocated
slowly staring in **each other's eyes** wide
gasping for air to put in our lungs
but there **wasn't any**

i imagined how much more would be available
if love weren't here
if it hadn't followed me **into this cube**
bitter. **i breathed,** asthmatic
i **wanted to be** in my box **alone**
confined, content + broken
where nobody could see

thoughts + pieces

the depths of **my wounds**
pledging my identity
to the pain i felt
never letting them heal
picking, scabbing
obsessing over things; **rehashing**
'til my heart was out of service **+ incapable**
of carrying what followed me
into this box
love

thought it would tire **of chasing me**
impatiently
giving up on ways
to make with me
but i was wrong. **it held on**
cramped in this crate
we talked for a few
listening to each other
be uncomfortable + true

i said, "love, i really **don't know**
what to do with you"
this box is too small
neither of us is leaving
either we both get out now
or together we stop breathing"
i waited + after minutes
of staring + nobody speaking
rotated my wrists. tightened fists
+ punched love in the face
to make **it start bleeding**
but love **punched back**
carefully **missing my chin** to hit the box
it cracked

that hole **brought in air**
that we both needed + light to see
how disfigured i was **from "box life"**
contorted joints; unable to extend right
the bruises left of love's arm

from holding me too tight
i brawled against love **never** hitting back
it absorbed every hit **+ beat the box**
after every attack
blow for blow; making **room to grow**
while i didn't know i needed to
violent + devoted
in hope + **hopeless**
in distance **+ closeness**
breathing freely + choking
love followed me
in a box
willing to die
with me or by my hand
love had **a plan**
to stay

drowning
***
your waves
ripple across my skin
in phases
states of matter
singular form
liquid
flowing together
we war but no one wins
i just learn **to swim**
drowning on most days
willingly

innately craving
the **bottom of a thing**
to explore it fully
losing myself + time
but it's worth it
for the view

thoughts + pieces

the question answered
or the rush that comes
from discovering something new
your power is wet
dripping **nutrient dense matter**
substance
carried **by**
the most essential
multi-dimensional
elements
hydrogen + oxygen. **mixed**
you **dissolve** me

distributing **my cells**
through your medium
structurally compromised
i am expanded.
i am purified
in your waves
i find **relief,** healing

thoughts + pieces

grief management, **peace**
love + action
breathing in me
that's where **i always want to be**
so i drown on most days
blissfully

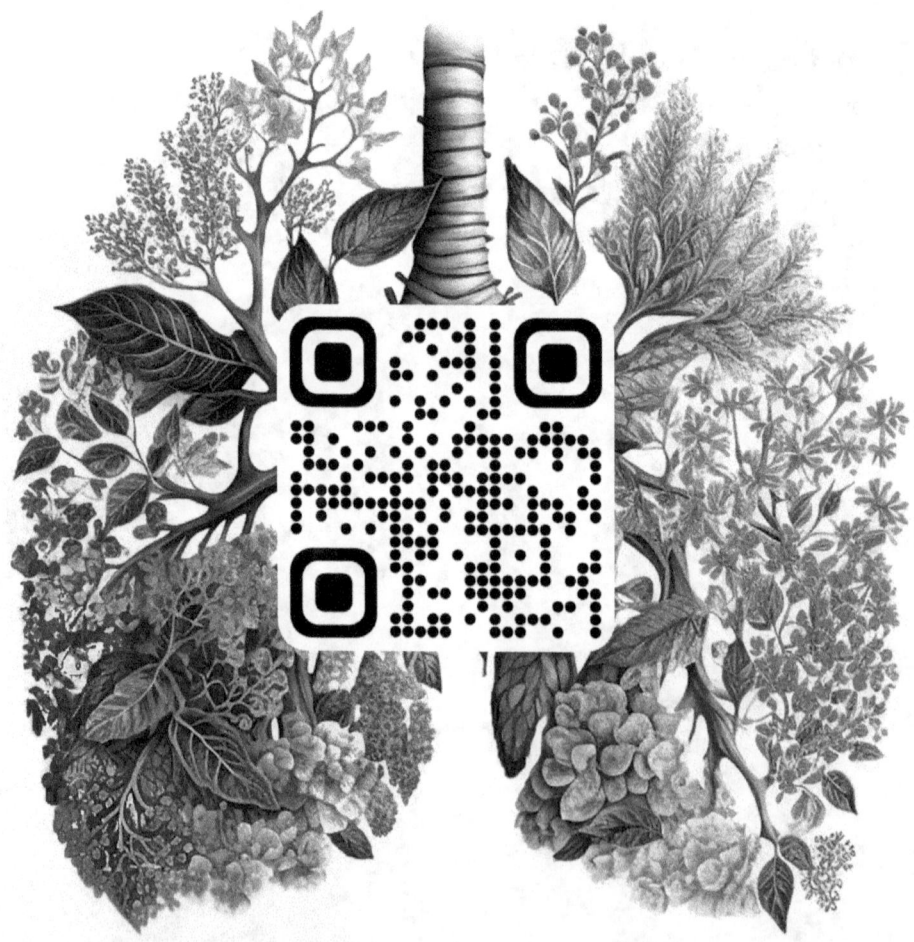

symptomatic

***

doc says
i'm symptomatic
this ache in my soul
won't ever go away
apparently **i'm coping**
with this space between
now + breathing
you
indefinitely

my air supply
eight hours + fifty-three minutes **away**
so i'm wheezing on most days
and nights typed deep
while sleep
i reek of **love's asthma**
can't catch my breath
because she has it

i left it **where i found a place to just be**
to just breathe and see
what's really possible
if i let go

die a little in her eyes + dream
the universe has a way **about these things**
+ sometimes
it likes to f*ck with me
intentionally
but i follow
take the hard pill **+ swallow**
poked + doped in doses
craving **closeness**
like iv dripping
ropes around my heart intact
in fact
carrying **contagious**
lingering artifacts
in skin to skin **+ back-to-back**

thoughts + pieces

contact
lymphatic
intrinsically her **addict**
actively relapsing with kisses
until i'm **asymptomatic**

for a moment, cured
healed **+ in remission**
until you leave again
or i leave you
and everything beautiful **i felt**
leaves me too
who aren't you?
if not a virus
consuming me **on occasion**
reframing my dna
that i **might** be
what love is
with **you**
this fever

thoughts + pieces

hasn't broken since
our first **conversation**
our first kiss
and the distance
keeps me **fighting off love** sickness
it's strange this pain
from separation **feels suitable**
crafting + carving out ways to keep
our love; **transmutable**

so i inhale our memories
rehab through **our laughs**
swim in your spirit
it makes the time pass
faster it seems
and i believe
this condition is different
its resilient + persistent
its big + bold; hard not to miss it
no lie

thoughts + pieces

i've never tried to resist it
letting it through
so doc i know
my symptoms are consistent

i am **coping**
self-diagnosing
opening + ecstatic
infected **with her love**
a symptom
addict

pay
attention

pay attention to snarky remarks
from the person you love.
it's not just witty banter
they are showing you things
they want seen.
notice them in real time.
create an opportunity to listen
with your mind open.

craving
***

this **moment**
this space in time
when we are **separate**
this feeling of wet emptiness
fills my soul
in a way **i've never known**
engorged with want
feels like fire
desire
+ misery
because your skin
miles apart from mine
who am i
without the **electricity**
between our epidermis
you charge me

kiss **my current**

shock this lust
tame + temper **this flame**
lay with me
from night until **eternity's dawn**
we'll **watch the sun on our bodies** in sweat
never letting this complex
test of "yes" puzzle us

sometimes a feeling
sometimes **a maze**
sometimes a moment
sometimes **a day**
sometimes right after
eyes gaze
not having you **is just as stimulating**
in this moment
in this feeling
i crave

long distance
***

your desire for me + incapability
in withstanding my absence **is not weakness**

the ache you feel sitting in the void of distance
between my heart, and yours **is not permanent**

the longing you have
the embarrassment of vulnerability
is not the scent of shame
it is the byproduct of meeting yourself
time and time again

**the echo of how others left
and stayed gone**
but this love is strong.

your feelings are a sign**, a proof
that everything now is right**

thoughts + pieces

everything now is divine
we have always been together
we caught up with time
now in it, our hearts want **to bend it**
patience **carries our love**
gently wrapping it in breathing + imagination

whenever **the pain**
in my heart craves
you **across my lips**
i drift
in future with you

existence **radiates**
with you closer
i shine with all my might
when **you are gone**
praying that "miles apart"
you feel my light
+ see the distance closing

thoughts + pieces

a house we made **a home**
writing stations with fruit
shea butter + lo fi music
a piece of **me and you**
merged
hearing birds sing
as we dance in the middle of the day + dream
whenever we're apart
imagine these things
as we write
in love + fight to trust
that one day **we'll wake up**
with only centimeters between
you + me

aroused

***

+ just like that **i was on fire**
completely consumed
drawn into **unknown depths**
sparks ignited + conducting
sending currents **to the soft + juicy**
delicate deliciousness **growing**
between my thighs
admiring
the ocean behind **those eyes**
jumping in **as tribute**
her volunteer **drowner**
just like katniss in hunger games
i play to win
+ swim so deep in you
that i get lost at sea
treading water **blissfully**

staying afloat

always ready to sink
ready to think
free + clear of **misconceptions**
open. wet. dripping
falling in **slow motion**
gripping
the back of my neck
slipping fingers across **my chest**
getting wet **never felt** this humid

lucidly **letting urges climb**
noticing everything twice
studying + storing **in real time**
drunken with possibilities + purpose
as she blossoms
in my fantasy's fantasy
climaxing
in my dream's dream
the most **beautiful concept**
to enter my mind

thoughts + pieces

in a long time
i'd wait **another thousand years**
just to think her
feverish + warm all over
satin sheets singing her praises
the thought of you **erases inhibition**
she's the aroma of past
bent on top of future
so familiar **and so new**
an energy i don't remember remembering
cause i feel like
i **already know you**

heat waves on my skin + pacing
she's invading **my lungs like air**
longing to be breathed
deeply, **slowly into each other's** mouths
before our soft lips become one
i plan to **put** her on me

not like a sweater or a crop tee
like a force field
controlling the weather in me
magnetized for thunderstorms **+ plenty** of showers
there's always a chance of rain
this drizzle could cool our fire
+ temper our **desire**
with more meaningful things like conversation
but words between us
a very dangerous combination
accelerated in **mental stimulation**
talk to me

while i sweat out
all the nasty things i want done
listening as **she hangs on syllables long enough**
for me to catch her tongue in action
she makes me **feel attraction**
whenever she enters the room
my temperature **gets harder to regulate**

so i hydrate everyday
just in case
you come around me
craving our next **encounter**
wet + wading
pulsating but patient
for all you might require
+ just like that **i was on fire**

today your eyes
***

today it's your eyes
every time i'm with you
i pick something new to obsess over
countless parts of you **intrigue me**
for a while now, **it's been your pinky**
definitely thought **about sucking it**
a time or two
i'm sorta...kinda ...into you

no...
like in you
inside **your body**
looking at me
smitten. **in awe of you**
magnificently in view; b-e-a-u-tiful
a treasure
i notice in every way
but today

thoughts + pieces

it's your eyes
they blind me **guiding** me closer
away from all the
pointless sh*t i obsess over
gasping at each blink
curiously watching you think

as your lids close
i sense **you leaving me**
only for a moment i know
a few milliseconds at the most
but my **love is fueled**
in moments with you
one lost is one less
one less is **one too many**

you look **like love**
meeting me on occasion
gazing. watching you
watching me

thoughts + pieces

never making it obvious
what it is you **think**
while staring
fixation generates sensations
stimulated

on warming your heart in glances
quiet laughs + taking chances
grasping at stars being **romantic**
building suits for time travel
to make love **on other planets**

galaxy wide
just like your eyes
round, **brown after kisses** dilated
opening, focusing
this portal for you
seated in view
of my eyes **feasting**
back on you

thoughts + pieces

in phases
hour long **gazes**
you are **consistently fascinating**
in **every** way
but today
it's your eyes

reminders
***
the smell of **lavender**
chance the rapper hits
trap music playlists
road trips + masego
open windows, **sunlight on skin**
the sound pens make on paper
ink bleeding into fiber
berry blend + mango **smoothies**
walks in the city
midday showers

reading books
profound enough to highlight
conversation
the rush of a new idea
having groceries **delivered**
sundays at ipanema

finding money hidden
the sound of a **cashapp notification**
vacation ideas
+ **unused** frequent flyer miles
the pulse of possibility
sitting in a room **customized**
like ikea
knowing there's a space
for my heart

dark shades of yellow
soft kisses + sweet breath
the cool of **tears falling away**
from my eyes
on both sides
down my face
circling my ears
the cut of silence from your voice
telling me
everything's gonna be ok

the space in lo-fi
the rhythm **of jazz**
the sway of hips
dancing at random
in the kitchen while cooking
giddy about "smashin' this food"

late night drives
rubs on thighs **+ prayer**
speaking to god as friend
listening to **all my feelings**
being asked questions
and noticed
for the purest parts of me
extra napkins in the bag
just in case or for "gp"

defying gravity
floating on **clouds + water**
the sprinkle of a splash

thoughts + pieces

uber eats **+ door dash**
luxury penthouse views
receiving **good news**
unexpectedly

successfully completing a secret handshake
coordinating outfits but not identical
being **seen**. becoming **new**
finding gold. **leaving clues**
discovering them **in you**

the impossibility in forgetting
the certainty **of keeping**
reminders

stay
visible

what if you stay visible? make it permissible to view. all of you. or does the light scare what confidence you have left? light grows all living things. are you living? take a deep breath. let the light in. allow it to bleed into every corner, every space and grow you.
stay visible.

RUMI

think/feel

feel the body
***

feel the body **i'm in**
all of its glory
it's **magnificent shape**
even the sound of cells moving
being **repaired**

feel the body **i'm in**
every space occupied
with who i am destined to be
my dreams
my peace
the reality **in each bone and muscle**
unused + developing

feel the body **i'm in**
every ache + pain
catches my attention
look at it

thoughts + pieces

carefully + closely
listen **to the smallest parts of me**
feel this body
arms that **have carried so much**
the burden of my heart
there are scars + marks
injuries and parts
that **i don't recognize** anymore
skin that hangs
from transforming
fat into muscle
breakdowns + break-ups
decoration **of earrings**
tattoos, lashes, and make up
accessorize this frame **in gold**
to mirror the shine within
having fun with **this body i'm in**

extend it to **other bodies**
grant their possession

blessed **with the gift** of my insertion
i'm certain
that it feels good **with me in it**
step into it fully
the body **is a tool**
you can jump into me
+ i can jump into you
sensing **each other**
learning what we've been through
i need you to fill me
i need to fill you
don't get confused
i'm talking to my body**, not you**
love will **make you merge** the two
what would you do **if i merged with you?**

i can guarantee bliss
anticipate pain
we'd have **dinner over obstacles**
+ kiss in the rain

thoughts + pieces

i'd shift reality
bringing **heaven** down
on wednesdays + thursdays
inside this body **is sacred**
i'm expecting **holy** sensations
learn how **to dance + romance** each body station
shower its brain **with stimulation**
for higher purposes + no explanation
occupy me **like i occupy myself**
fill it up to the brim
until **there's nothing left**
but space to **overflow**
into healing
feeling
this body i'm in

humans have faces
***
humans have faces
that change at will
for real
watch how eyes roll
corners of mouths stretch wide
innocent smiles + scheming
calculating the chance
in a glance
up + down, scanning my body
to let me know you like what **you see**

my frame in your pupils
dilate the mystery
biting your lip **anticipating**
how my energy tastes
it tastes like me
but the senses you use
to encounter me on this plane

are subpar at best
i'm a quest
you can't conquer me in a glance
or even begin to know **if i**
am **what you** like
but keep trying
staring to remain in my good graces
but **humans have faces**
that change at will
for real

watch how jaws clench
when anger floods the veins of a lover
but under covers
eyes close + exhales fill the room with desire
an aroma more contagious than corona
unvaccinated
have you been contemplating?
whether it's lust, love, or a pattern of convenience
to not look into the soul of your lover

thoughts + pieces

as you press your body
across the skin of another being
that's seeing
slow it all the way down
until its observation
we become one
+ sex is like masturbation
we get off on good communication
get familiar with each other's spaces
cause **humans have faces**
that change at will
for real

watch how shade
gets thrown so easy
if it doesn't look like you, act like you
or stimulate your mind
you won't find a space to put it
even though most of us are empty enough
to spare a corner

we judge for fun
posting for the likes
pressured by the opinions
and it's dangerous
to put it out if you can't take it
but i wonder if we'd stop to see
how we're already naked
how we all know how to fake it
if maybe
our faces
would remain
+ we could actually see each other
discover what **we** like
who **we** are, how **we** life
together + embrace it
but **humans have faces**
that change at will
for real

the masks we wear like a tattoo

permanent
we hold that *thang*
we nurture it
taking care of its needs like it's really me
cause everybody got one
+ if i take mine off
i don't want to be the only
social but lonely
depression the mainline
impression the main lie
confession i can't hide
the power to express in divine time
like right now
while your face is changing
thinking of how exposed you'd be
if we saw you **at will, for real**
the reflection of what's inside
a connection with your true light
it's a blessing we keep hoarding
at any space + time

we could stop
looking at faces that **aren't really** you
but only if you want us to
humans have faces
that change at will
for real

watch how wrinkles appear
scars tell stories + keep hostage
images in our mind
of how things **should** be

you are in a body
human
with a face
in an experiment
on a timer
you'd better pace
+ make the most of this space
you call home for now

thoughts + pieces

time will change your face
anyhow
be real while you're here
show some you
i'm scared too
that just means i'm
human for real
changing at will
with my face
like you

making
friends

opportunities to socialize will come.
you don't have to run. leave when you need to
+ lean into spaces of growing authentically.
at some point these walls need to dissolve.
you've fortified enough + your light isn't blocked.
just hidden but leaking. peeking out
+ seeking view behind the walls in
perfect timing. stop hiding.

space
***

taken in doses + swallowed
forcefully
down **+ through the tube**
that leads to digestion
its medicine
the **kind tasted** + endured

stretching out **the vibe in branches**
chanting mantras **+ dancing**
there's room to grow; **alone i say**
with company **maybe; but** it shaky

dangerously inserted at will
it feels prescribed **like pills**
killing almost **everything** to save some

chemo for those emotionally stunted
in radioactive decay **+ half-life**
its half-right; **we half-fight** ourselves
cause the winner **also injures**
+ hurt needs someone to blame
while standing **in the mirror**
searching + scouting out
the identity of the offender
while also looking at **him or her**
it's absurd

unseen
since **there's space between**
you **+ me**
the distance **of my reflection**
looking back
totals our imperfections in truth

thoughts + pieces   53

if **it's me**; **then** it's also you
+ this space **doesn't make us** invisible
so why are we acting; **hologram-ish**
it's awkward
space

placed in the category "necessary"
but is it? really?
the final frontier
for nebulas + planets
in human connection
space is typically **a sign of damage**
someone feels smothered
or fears losing themself
+ that need to hide
from you **seeing me** see myself

privacy's so selective

i've seen **more vulnerability**

in captions than conversation

+ the comments

are an even deeper situation

we bare our **souls under anonymity**

away from everyone we know **+ in our own**

space is finicky

gimmicky can literally

swing **either way**

one minute **a safe haven**

and the next a perfect getaway

from closeness **open**

can't tell if we're digesting slow **or chokin'**

from smokin' the mirrorstell me how to swing it

+ where to place this space

i'll listen

can't i want you all the time

+ not be codependent

let's align our definition

+ cling to each other **in distance**

create a spot **just for us** in the center

space to explore

space to **enjoy separate**

together

energy diet
***
what does your spirit eat?
does it feed **energetically**
digesting what it hears
absorbing **through eyes**
or rotting in minds
from the filth **we've seen**
+ things **spoken over** us

"**flat tummy tea**" your brain
+ purge, **try it**
put your life on an energy diet
filter the **environments**
you lay, stay, + play in
take vitamins
of truth **+ chew**

swallow them slow
to protect you **from you**
not **paying attention**
its detrimental + it **has symptoms**

comparison **inconsolable**
urges uncontrollable
delusions + **time wasted**
"going through the motions" **+ "faking it"**
always tired
there are deficiencies in your diet
when was the last time **you were inspired?**
to invest in some feat
to sit down **in a space + breath** in peace
to **curate** a routine
of **monitoring habits**
to discover what's making you

sick + tired
of being silent
you can keep quiet but try it
put your life
on an **energy diet**

thought
***

you **are** not **here**
you just think you are
and it's **that thought**
that **lies to you** and with you
till you are no more **than a thought**

what you were from the beginning
it couldn't possibly be that simple
or so you **thought**
wrong, maybe,
quickly replaced **by the next**
thought

like high school beef, **childhood grief**
and all those things that you no longer believe
abandoned

thoughts + pieces

after you became aware
of the mind's discovery
that **it** carries what **it is** + you **are**
thought

not just of but in + through
out of his **came you**
a thought
nothing more
might not be what you were hoping for
but you now know eternity's secret
that **you are**
thought

it **cannot** die
it cannot **miss**
it **cannot** be unthought

thoughts + pieces

it is **and it lives**
never beginning **or ending**
thoughts

when **thought** fully
are glimpses of what it felt like before you
as it formed **complete and unique**
separate from any other previous thought
it peaks with imagination
shines in **frustration's view**
think about it
but you're already thinking
without having to tell you to

you do **what you are**
you are what you do
+ this thought **is speaking life to you**

thoughts + pieces

wants to **creep** in you

sink in you

drop down **deep**

sleep + blink in you

something **tangible**

but i can't **wrap my hands** around it

for a long time i thought about it

kept thinking **that if i thought** i was

thinking i wasn't

a thought **must've slipped in**

thinking in sin

i thought the unthinkable

that i am **something**

not formed by the process of thinking

rationalizing that i **was something more** or less

not a thought

thoughts + pieces

maybe a thing
and that made me **second guess**
and if true, makes me here
and i am **not**
i just think i am
sometimes

i'm **currently learning** to think
ideas + not time,
abundance + **not hoarding** thoughts
i'm afraid to let go
junking my brain, **constrained** in logic
expounding on things that can't be explained
its pain that i feel **+ i cause**
i am **the only problem** i'm here to solve

today i **think pass thought**

thoughts + pieces

for a more comprehensive view
cause **my thought** is that
on **the other side of think** is "do"
everything impossible
that i feel called to

i think free **while thoughts fly**
experimenting in action
while the fear in me **thinks about what could**
i make moves to see what *might actually* happen
investigating every case of doubt with faith
getting bold with my brain's
similarity to god's
i think **+ he dreams**
i dream + he thinks
in waves hoping that
i'll find + stay in his frequency

thoughts + pieces

its clearer to me **when we think together**

god **rarely** gives me answers
but always **thoughts to remind me**
where to find them
god thinks now
what i'll see **eventually**
myself

as **this thought** comes to be
for a moment in life, but **a constant in eternity**
thinking **itself** in perpetuity
and **being** what it is
an idea of God
like the moon **and stars**
in skies **high + dark,** beaming
we are **intentionally magnificent**

works of art in thinking
about itself in **beings**
keeping thought clear
we **are not** here
we just think
we **are**

be
honest

be honest. with you. first.
tell the truth to your heart + mind.
listen. pay attention. do not ignore.
accept the gift of being able
to talk to yourself. hear the words.
say them to yourself.
listen again and breathe.

church baby

RUMI

god, weed, + ptsd
***

the book of life

chapter 3

god, weed, and ptsd

99% of the symptoms

came post trauma

like 30 years after seeing the monster in daddy **get bigger**

and take a bite out of mamma

i found pieces of her in **hymns + songs**

blood-stained walls + crying all night

crust in eyes + loopy

still remembering things

i never wanted to see

like bugs crawling in the dark

pillows on floors in closets

while terror **roamed our home**
torturing the womb
that carried me
she taught me **god does crazy things**

like nothing at all
it's crazy to me
cause **i thought god knew everything**
if i was god and i knew
that man would put **his hands on you**
+ 2 little black girls who weren't abused
would carry the symptoms past age 32
i'd be ok with a jay or two
it'd definitely be permissible
i'd sit with you
through girl scout cookies, og kush + gorrilla glue
healing's a crazy thing too

thoughts + pieces

what it looks like for me
might be different for you
but never any condemnation
cause i got **the revelation**
after i stopped segregating
putting distance **between god + me**
when its god & weed
killing the ptsd

at least having me **less symptomatic**
in basket of bad dreams i keep havin'
so with every toke
the nightmares plays **but the sound is off**
and when god talks to me
i'm not alone when the lights on

seeing what's hidden

afraid to admit it
system glitches + **quick fixes in a pinch**
they never see me flinch from loud noises
that don't exist any more
cause my brain's **chain to memory**
extends further than me
tightening around my suffering
creeping into me on sundays
so it feels safer to **worship online**
and maintain my blend of
spirit, substance + syndrome
incubated by his grace + her mercy

i don't need you to validate my medication
never an addiction, **a holy prescription**
some days i'm just trying to keep my head above water
the waves bring stress. **post trauma.** disorder

but i'm faded **falling fixed at his feet**
grieving, sleeping, **keeping light on me**
photosynthesizing things rooted deep
growing, slowing, flowing effortlessly
healing is a specialized blend for me
of god + consistency

fragmeant

***

my life

my whole life

is lived **in pieces**

and parceled

like ladles of **chicken noodle**

souped to those starving

for power it seems

power over me

or at least **the piece** given

in the mornings

i assess each piece

removing debris

documenting damages

processing claims **with god**

he rarely asks
why his creation is so self-abusing
that she's allotted her whole
to become half
depends on who's in the room
or who might be watching
what they might say
or might think
i sink

deeper in this place of "meant"
where my programming
expresses intent
divide to survive
knife to wrist.
down one inch
be everything to everyone

that's it
force yourself to be digested
that's sick
there are layers to this sh*t
fragment

so i fit in the box **better**
covered in blood
tattered
jagged + ragged matter
plastered on actors
fumbling **as all** in the world
constantly tempted to slice
bite size + die
slow
It's all **i know**
maybe that's an excuse

but what else am i supposed to do

maybe it's meant
maybe **it's me**
maybe it isn't possible to be
a whole

in my mind
hands over my eyes
blocking me from **seeing**
the knife in my heart
infected
unresponsive to **antibiotics**
void of hope
desperate
functioning **in separate**
pieces

thoughts + pieces

pieces meant for **pain**
pieces meant to collide
i remember
building this chop shop at five
when i saw how much
everybody lies

practice your lines
make sure **you sound happy**
make sure it sounds like you
fake it '**til you make it**
if you do
it's probably **only**
a piece of you

lost like the rest of us
grinding

thoughts + pieces

who we are into crumbles
our chunks are too hard
to stomach

nobody's whole
just decent
fragmented
into bigger pieces
can't remember the last time
i was a big piece of me

frag:
meant to be myself
meant to be strong

frag:
meant to speak up

thoughts + pieces

+ not just go along

frag:
meant to **find out why**
meant to get help

frag:
meant to cut me up
+ **lose myself**

disassembled
so many times
i'm comfortable **broken**
weak days + **weekends**
more or less **socially** slicing
my entire life in
pieces moving fast

thoughts + pieces

talkin crazy like
yesterday i went
pieces talk half
in thoughts **incomplete**
a glimpse of a soul that used to be

whole
together
in one room
now alone
in pieces
muttering prayers
to self-destruct
watching god
reconstruct
kissing each piece
in amazement

thoughts + pieces

his creation
if i had his eyes
then **maybe**
i'd see some light
remember what whole
used to feel like

god to me

***

my god
doesn't have a gender
or a race
he/she/it is trans
formative
+ i am form forming

my god listens to me
+ **loves questions**
we argue sometimes
i've never had a win
but i've never lost
it's not a battle
we spar
in a ring

inside of this **grayish pink** thing
it's wrinkly, but it works
whenever god gives me **her point of view**
my brain hurts
stretching to meet
the ideal phenomena of possibility
my god is **a shared** commodity
so i say "my" **as a term of endearment**
not truth
my god love people that look like me
my god loves people **that look like you**
my god whispers too

in the wind + the waves of water
in mercy shown
when you didn't deserve it
in this planet, **and the oxygen it provides**

for all of us to be breathing
right now
my god is all about
taking it down
looking **around**
+ seeing
making human
beings

my god is on the fence **about the "g"**
whether it's capitalized or not
depends on the day of the week
+ whether or not **you know him like that**
my god is not grammatical
my god is **beyond language**
words are just useful
when you're his creation

but i get bored **from anticipation**
jump headfirst into experimentation
+ play with energy
center in myself, **open the portal** in my heart
so god can get into me

not because of what i said
because of who i am
a home built of muscle tissue + ideas
a soul **so in love with the life** he gives
she's his
she's **hers**
present for all the nouns
consumed **in all the verbs**

my god **acts, loves,** waits
gives, **saves, pleases**, takes

sings, protects, dates
+ romances on occasion
i feel like **his favorite**
my knight in shining savior
my god **rescues**
he's **that** dude
+ so patient

my god rocks with me
while i'm playing
giving more time
while i waste it
i'm grateful
my god is able
to deal with me

my god suitable **for my delusion**

allowing me **to think free** + dream
see, be, + cling
to things **that don't make sense**
+ have discussions with me
about it
he already knows + stays quiet
while i search **for the answers**
right in front of my face
never i told you so

my god is the single most
important thing to my brain
+ existence **on this plane**
of earth in this system
i'm not ashamed to admit it
i know **where my help comes from**
+ what it looks like

it looks like **my god**
in **my life**
at all times

not because i'm right **or perfect**
because he likes me
everything included
flaws and all
my god wants to be involved
the walls **in my heart aren't** permanent
they protect the space
reserved for the being **that allows me to**
breathe + be with ease
god to me **is god with me**
talking + listening
experiencing life **as + in** each other
swimming in the substance **of dreams**

thoughts + pieces

creating things
love + synergy
god to me
is everything

show + tell

***

if i had the **courage**

i'd show you **how bruises stain**

screams silenced resonate in behaviors

condensing into liquid; viscous

gathered in a spoon to become a syringes greatest

companion

inserted **in veins and sorted** by actions

a few minutes of bliss; drooling

if i had the **truth**

i'd show you **how hiding drains**

to slow to notice how comfortable you make the dark

using fingers **to feel the shapes** of things

forgetting to breathe **when footsteps approach**

closeness smells like danger

ears make up **stories, hearing voices**

thoughts + pieces

the pressure of silence pokes a hole
dripping drops of paranoia; fooling

if i had **faith**
i'd show you **how church is a maze**
where players use prayers to play god
people get exchanged **like currency. currently**
sold out on being told what to think
intellect traded in **for titles**
pastors become bibles
reading humanity
leaving you **starving for the divine**
hoping to be **a winner**
in a race god never sanctioned
panting, **out of breath,** running for years
"drinking the koolaid", making strides
on a hamster wheel

thoughts + pieces

going nowhere
except **weekly services** + "facebook live's"
knowingly broke. cheerfully tithe
to a system **where god has favorites**
+ delivers **based upon your seed**
when **you could** just read
for yourself + breathe
bask in the sun + be. free
to think with god; schooling

if i had **peace**
i'd show you **how fear tames**
playing freeze tag with your brain
dreams, **hot** cold **then frozen**
echoes of pain from being open
ran through **like plastic cups**
they show up at every party

+ left for someone else **to clean up**
famished
fear scavenges for the light in you
god's perfect container
blemished + all, he paused
+ called time into you
but **fear is aware of everything**
you are not paying attention to
it swaps out thoughts **+ speaks to you**
typically **right before** action
or as a distraction
your effort **is what fear is after**
so act **in spite of** its claims
healing through bruises **in staying**
beating the odds + not weighing
the validity **of your** placement
a star in its place shining; ruling

thoughts + pieces

they told me to wait

***

out the gate

a prize promised

to the highest bidder **for my holiness**

i wanted to be won

so i **buried my urges**

a virgin

purged for purpose + worth marrying

having babies with **and claiming**

i knew my place

a sanctified bride, quiet

graciously good **at fake**

they told me to wait

so saving myself

i let my mind wander

in all **the empty spaces** of religion

thoughts + pieces

finding so much bullsh*t, "off" sh*t
code switch **+ nonsense**
barely believable systems
in place to **program gender**
steer sexuality **+ speak for god** in preference
i saw performance + stage
love that only showed up
when people were watching
disappearing **through walls** at home
conjured up **for the kids** + family gatherings
masters of **masking + saving face**
they to me to wait

but i had questions about what i was saving
is it this flower **between my thighs?**
or the thoughts i have in my mind?
am i waiting to be "next in line" **for the love i'd seen?**

thoughts + pieces

don't i get to decide **for me?**
what does "**chaste**" mean?
cause at night i think all sorts of freaky things
body parts i want **touched, rubbed, licked** + bitten
with this "v" card + his d*ck hard
my **hormones losing sight** of the mission
felt guilty for what **my body** needed
started **suppressing desires** for jesus
to get closer to me
if i did **what they said**, he'd give me a mate
they told me to wait

so i did
but i had conditions **+ coping strategies**
i could only kiss a boy + he could touch
kiss my neck **or rub my butt**
he couldn't cum **but i could**…with myself

i played in ways **i never imagined**
messed up a lot of sheets
disconnecting completely discovering me
self-pleasure **was my thing**
to keep me out of danger
sacred + exclusively available for a stranger
i'd marry + submit to
after **"i do"**
at the altar
locked the decision in place
while masturbating **every day**
they told me to wait

made it through 26 cycles around the sun
super horny + settling **for an op i thought best**
but just conveniently in the same space
stressing + suppressing **over and under** everything

barely holding out
for a chance to release **the sexual tension**
under god's law
first encounter
4 out of 5 buckets of trash
it was bad
sad **that i thought** it was **supposed** to be
only about him **being pleased**
sex + my sexual expression
had never been about me
i was a professional at fake
masking **straight-faced**
pleasing was my duty **but pleasure** never mine
pulling away to finish off **while he slept**
snoring through my pleas **for other things**
+ our need for therapy in discussion
but **ignored**

thoughts + pieces

forged ahead **accepting my fate**
he told me i was too much
they told me to wait

i was patient, **kept waiting**
had already loss what i was saving
contemplating **why my sacred**
was so adjacent **to my placement**
in society, church + husbands **needing wives**
broken. **disappointed**
angry. pissed
so wait a minute god… i waited for this
is there someone **i can speak to**
cause i feel invisible
without my vagina
or my **wedding ring**

if i did what i was told

why didn't it work out for me?

was it a **mistake**? to **wait**

maybe it was safe

or bait

to **keep me in a place** of

forfeiting decisions

transforming **under opinions**

as my reasonable service

but furthest **from god's original purpose** + design

deep down inside feels like i wasted time

so pressed for holy

only did what **they told me**

to wait

head homes

your head is not a home.
it's a place. **but we do more than visit.**
we "stay-cay" for days, **camping out on**
thoughts, replaying scenes + outcomes,
making **temporary permanent.**
your mind is only one **of the**
many spaces to be. you can always
return to your mind. leave sometimes.

RUMI

leaking dark

trackstar
***

i run away from things
that **seem too good for me**
too good to be
sustainable
as my heart composts
organic material **unfertilized**
a 50:50 mix of hope and disappointment
so, i water my **dreams + trauma**
healing and disease in the same garden
'cause i keep running
even when my legs tire
i fire up my **appetite for escape**
in place of **tracing the lines**
of excuses, broken promises + **wastes of time**
not honoring my true self
i need help

thoughts + pieces   111

but help 'gon have to chase me
cause i'm off + running
full speed, hard like rocks
every time my feet hit the ground
my brain stops being confused
no longer thinking; i'm immune
impermeable to the **fumes** of **toxic sh*t**
i didn't ask for this. **i was six**
+ maybe you were only 8 or 12
now were adults **running from heaven**
'cause… well
it feels too good
+ we're convinced that **behind every good moment**
are three terrible ones
so we **run professionally**
self-sabotaging olympians
medals of withdrawal, **plaques of isolation**

coming in first place at the race
to safety in separation
that's who we are
trackstars
grammy-award winning
head spinning
masters of **vanishing**
panicking
holistic holograms
damaging tracks

stars with trust issues
leveraging our shine
waiting for the ball to drop
out of **the sky**
in lanes painted, stretching **for the next 4 x 4**
nesting in starter blocks like **birds**

selling wings for two knees
hoping to see more faster
running from no one
chasing ourselves in circles
never captured
cycling the **same emptiness**
that abandoned you
leaving yourself **to soothe + coo**
in cribs long after being a baby
evidence of "malnutur-ing" you
absence **is what we're used to**

stars **escape + exits** on our terms
it burns
but **we let it** for the scars
these marks keep us out of retirement
+ training for **relays in relationships**

dating sprints
casually looking up marriage tips
afraid to stay in something
long enough **to choose**
presence, confronting, showing up
+ trying something new
tracking **fidgety**
emotionally **configuring**
happiness is triggering
altering calculations **of how damaging**
humans can be
what if they see me **+ leave**
will i always run away from things
that **seem too good** for me
too good to be
sustainable

my story

***

my story **didn't matter**
not enough **drama**
in my trauma to cause chatter + tweets
on pages **+ screens**
featuring me
as myself **doing basic things**
basically
i dealt with **dealing**
+ healing alone

my story was **an existential repeat**
a **carbon copied echo** from recycled history
of a black. **girl.** losing. **magic**
weighing her struggles
against world hunger + sexual abuse
feeling bad for feeling sad
about the **non-life-threatening** things

she'd been through

my story **was concealed + neatly tucked**
was never **touched**
but **constantly** disappointed
psychologically hijacked
in a chokehold **with "perfect" performance**
leaving marks mostly invisible + **hard to see**
you'd need **cognitive microscope** to know
how **little things** affect me
in **big ways**
like the smell of **cologne**
on good days
pulling up memories of having a father **+ being a kid**
but underneath that same aroma
is the stench of **abandonment**

my story was **a consecrated contradiction**
where sanctuaries **feel like gravy, poured on thick**
to **make addicts** look like pastors

+ moving forward **going backwards**
seers looking away, women **learning their place**
i saw quiet tolerant faith
where "meek and lowly" **meant holy**
+ a greater chance of being chosen
by a man **and the system that needed** me broken
left me **choking on holiness**
as a hostage in mother's dream
stuck in scenes of daddy's nightmare
where i couldn't scream
where stories were held to save face
buried under his mercy + grace
it was biblical
catch **me at church**, it's a miracle
'cause my **deepest distress** consistently came
from **someone spiritual**

my story was a "lose-win"
cause my **bruises; they blend** in
concealing ideations **of not being**

thoughts + pieces   **1 1 8**

important *enough* for view
convincing me to convince myself
to **formulate a rule**
not to share the details
of a story that **couldn't** matter
it was common, covered, **and confusing**
leaving my **heart + mouth** closed
my purpose **inactive**
making silence attractive

my story **had chains + cages**
with all sorts of people
a varying assortment of places
and more than enough pages
that i didn't write
my story **had a life**
of its own, **that i lived in third person**
watching things happen to me
but i wonder **what my story could be**
if i wrote it

thoughts + pieces

with my plot + my twists
if I told it
forgetting **about the pages
of any other story** but mine
until it matters

disappearing
***
for days where **my biology**
misaligns with time
in hindsight
reflexes + inflection
tone**. perception**
thoughts swarming **around me**
i'd pay blood to shut my brain off

heavy. caged
patient by force, **restricted**
limited range of motion
was hoping
but **there's nothing i can do**
so i won't. i don't
i am **not here**
disappearing

inhale but no ex
the breath i took in last
turned **on itself**
choking up the truth
of everything i've felt
and it feels ugly
what i buried grew
blooming **in all i do**
busting through stone walls
rock hard **of hearing**
from four feet under ground
+ currently **disappearing**

but i outlined me
in **something** somewhat **recognizable**
a charming personality quite identifiable
while hiding in plain sight + dying **in view**

eroding in fear; **bound**
by what **it was programmed** to do
possessed by a variety of anxieties
never speaking up + covering what's inside of me
socially **i look whole**
rehearsing motions **to go through**
grabbing glimpses
picturing **pictures**
tracing me
drawing lines + coloring outside **boundaries**
skeptical of visible
questioning **my engineering**
regularly disappearing

slowly **fading to black**
in increments
turning the knob **from left to right**

thoughts + pieces

experimenting with my existence
in every room **flicking switches**
setting dark to light
death to fight
jabbing the notion **that i am not worth** seeing
peeking at a masterpiece
draped in **societal expectations**
met time + time again
except they are not **mine**
just passed on with general **admission**
apparently
it comes with the ticket
but i'm here for the show
to watch, to learn, **and to grow**
not under a microscope
through **eyes of love** + arms of safety
longing to be **accurately perceived**

that's why i'm slowly **fading**

so notice my shifts + remember **i'm healing**
listen to my **view + investigate** my feelings
don't get tired when you can't **figure me out**
try again because i'm worth it
i'm hiding **because i'm hurting**
from pain i cannot name
but love could erase the shame
softening this shell **into a portal**
not so far, always nearing
+ possibly **reappearing**

needles + chord changes

***

burnt spoons **in hands gifted**
fitted to play g minor 13
wide enough for keys
but not wide enough to be seen
at least not for real
it was death by collaboration
we saw **your eyes**, your intoxication
that doped-out gaze, **drooling**
constant hospitalization
+ when it was...
they showed up for visitation
with the **same wide eyes** of glorification
the ground you walked on **got worship**
your daughters got 1/4 of you
minimum wages
needles + chord changes

thoughts + pieces

missed out + pleading
skin cracked + bleeding
breathing deeply
with dreams seeping through floors
one of fifteen
somewhere **somehow**
you got into some things
unattended
left to cultivate + cover
in dark corners you tampered with others
writing sin in songs on holy pages
needles + chord changes

modulations in half-step progressions
god's gifts mixed in with your obsessions
coagulated **+ clotted in veins**
arteries collapsed from clear view

i hate the blindfold we put on for you
with the talent came silence, few told you the truth
so in awe of what came out, even less looked **into you**
afraid of what we'd see
afraid of what you'd do
musical revolutionary **+ conduit of abuse**
i still feel pain from things i **didn't** do
because of you

sharp + famous. **aimless**
nowhere for this anger to go
but dangerous rows
a planted seed **without water**
always had a dad
never felt like a daughter

the sound of you playing

thoughts + pieces 129

still rings in my ears sometimes
crippling my heart
cause i feel you in light + on stages
having books of songs unpublished
free to roam **but i keep them in cages**
what if success makes me like you
+ the gifts i have **mix with obsessions too**
i fell in love with music **but i hated you**
my feeble attempt at balance
became an addict **to everything you left**
me, **my dreams,** and possibility

sorting through **memories of you**
like a bushel of apples picked from a garden
surrounded by a swamp
that gets plenty of rain **+ little sun**
even the ones that look ripe **ain't worth eating**

cause i know what they grow from

needles made us grow out of reach
but i always hoped **you'd get to me**
competing with the serum in your system
i watched life **leak out of you**
staining your legacy in shame
making it a **burden to bear** your name
but the gift remains
in life's songs
chords always change

so i take up instruments **to learn** sound
singing in every key
surrendering to higher powers
chords changing me
the tracks you left on your arms

thoughts + pieces

are in my head now
cleansing + clearing my view of what you were
a blend of perfection + error
public god; **private terror**
a talent ended too soon
the reason i stick to good people
who don't let me get consumed
i'll never **be like you**

to needles
i was an unworthy contestant
robbed of a **whole** person
your life short. **my long** lessons
divinely uneven exchanges
needles + chord changes

like sh*t
***
you made me feel
like sh*t
and i let you
flush my effort to love well
selling my soul
for shoddy attempts at reciprocation
one-sided convos. **hesitation**
bottom-shelf sex + masturbation
not sure **what** it was
but it wasn't love we were making
i still performed
knowing you liked **that moan i'd do**
it was never you

just **me**
making **you**
feel **like**
sh*t...something

thoughts + pieces

cause when i looked **into your eyes**
i knew you weren't
but i tried
to make you **the promise**
cramming your piece **into my puzzle**
forcing fit
+ from a distance
the picture **looked great**
nods + attention
"yall look so good together"
smiles + well wishes
hearts…likes… mentions
when you're in it, sh*t feels different
far away **will have you tricked**
everything that looks right
doesn't fit
like…
sh*t…
half of the people **i've been with**
i was *that* girl

thoughts + pieces

the one who stayed **conceptually**
it pleased me to have
something
temporarily even
physically encountered; **mentally alone**
neglected + controlled
unprotected
prey for every demon they carried
+ desperate **to fix the picture**
away from view
so the next time they saw us together
i'd *actually* **feel blessed** to be with you

i bottomed out on fixing
you wore my soul **down to the bone**
becoming **everything** you wanted **+ none of me**
served **every morsel of goodness** i had to you
while eating **processed food,**
cold, **lazy,** half-ass effort
bullsh*t reasons **why you don't love** like i do

thoughts + pieces   **1 3 5**

but i **got over my trauma** for you
buried **every excuse** to tally up
what we each put on our table
+ when i shared my needs
you made me feel **like sh*t**
ungrateful
discarded
something used **to wipe**
+ make yo a** feel nice
i'm a "**right**" you **wronged.** fixed
gulped not sipped
honorably dismissed
+ presently evolving **past like**

in **light beams** fertilizing **soil**
flowering streams of **letting go**
+ letting love take root
growing **through**
weeds **you planted**
you make me feel

like dancing
cause **what i felt** from you
was **never truth**
just a projection
to blind you **from you**
you made me **feel like** what i allowed **you to**
+ i'm responsible
for leaving **how i feel about me** in your hands
what i feel like
will never be regulated by another person again
+ like glue
this lesson **'gon stick**
never. will i ever
let anyone
make me feel
like sh*t

thoughts + pieces

RUMI

dreams + things

righting writing

***

i write out of love
i right in love
i write over love
i **right through** love
sitting beside it
as she watches me
i bait love to write on me

to carry words resting
at the bottom of my soul
up through veins + intellect
intersecting with ideas
in my chest and out
breathing
seeping through ink in skin
tattooed **+ bleeding** on paper
staining outside **the lines**

thoughts + pieces

no guides, or "how-tos"
all is always **right with you**

presently **righting**
in friendlier skies
floating + growing on cloud 9i
can't divide
imaginary with numbers
writing vision
love **plus intention**
equals me; "**mathing" different**
+ at angles
so that writing with "w"
+ right with "r" are interchangeable

seamlessly **cross defined**
keeping context **on both sides**
cause writing rights me in love
+ in writing love **possesses**
it confronts by protection

writing tests
my **desperation for release**
to do what i feel
practice what is free
i write from love's demand
to let me be
the paper, the ink, the pen
even the blanks to fill in
writing is listening to me
putting cracks in my walls
sharing intimately
with you
righting **is the move**

allowing theories to self-correct
giving the heart a mirror **to inspect**
for scars
hardening **soft tissue**
acts of wrong
longing to right

thoughts + pieces

written in honest
innately nocturnal
disinterested in **journals**
i write at night on screens
i right on write **to the extreme**
rectifying things
looking deep
inside myself **on purpose**
when it hurts, i write in the pain
write up through my veins + intellect
intersecting with ideas
in my chest and out
breathing
seeping through ink in skin
tattooed **+ bleeding** on paper
staining outside **the lines**
no guides, or "how-tos"
all is always
write with you

where's the machine?

***

where's the machine
that builds dreams
out of systems failing
the songs of ailing people
witnessing injustice
three miles to whole foods, **using coupons**
discounted living
ripping at the seams
where's the machine

that builds dreams
over dead bodies left in the street
yellow line. homicide
cases dropped **like shells from police**
standard issue pistols + protocol for skin
under the look away **of government**
conveniently blinded

policy makers who've never lived
where murder is sanctioned with ease
where's the machine

that builds dreams
through an identity lost on ships
beaten down to **microscopic pieces** with whips
trolling
chains that keep us
scrolling + comfortable
posting
posing for cameras
hosting parties **instead of gardening**
feasting on screens
"dream-like" illusions
we keep producing broken humans
stuck. cookie cut
type-casted for the scene
where's the machine

that builds dreams
with doubt
alongside "figuring it out"
in minds that are conscious, aware + streaming
struggling with the truth + scheming
an algorithm to find mechanisms outdated
erase + replace them with something greater
a machine
that cultivates dreams out of everything
composting prejudice + distraction
with self-love + interactions
with **new people**, new places, **new scenes**
by all means

it is necessary
to code fast
temper glass + close ad
reel watching. **real fast**
digitally feeding on real trash
side effects loading

coasting. **covering ears**
strengthening gears with limited exposure

learning to think in dreams
confronting **any impossible thing**
with faith, questions
+ courage to fuel investigation
a sophisticated machine of imagination
the **brilliance beneath** pain unseen

an innovation of **hope**
in becoming the machine
that builds dreams

protect her
***

i just want to protect her
engineer a force field around her light
a filter for eyes to sift out comparison
so she never forgets how beautiful she is
as herself
she'd scroll **under this protection**
feast on unconditional affection
there's nothing she has to do ever
for my attention

i just want to **protect her**
make our safe spaces
her favorite places to be
opportunities to scream
cry in peace
to let go + see treasures **in her being still**
eagerly willing to seek out the deep

thoughts + pieces

boldly **embracing the new**
i would stay aware of her
make friends with angels
+ invite them to walk with her
by the **intention**
of gods infinite wisdom
i'd send support **for comfort** on difficult journeys
turning corners + back tracking
i would trace her steps
remind her why she left
expose her heart **to something else**

cause i just want to **protect her**
from **wasting time**
second-guessing her intuition
+ making **everybody else happy**
i'd write **"you matter"** on sky lines
and **"this is for you"** in sunshine
i'd sing songs about her
humming **in the same frequency** used to craft her frame

thoughts + pieces

sounds would pour out of me **to soothe her mind**
aid her sleep
she'd rest on **things impossible**
+ believe
whatever she dared to take on **i'd fuel**
at every altar, **i'd wed her**
+ let it be known

that i just want to **protect her**
not for the fear of dangerous things
i know what she holds
how her value causes envy
she often gets **distracted**
in fixing people who lust for her light
she fights
to prove herself wrong **but she's right**
again + again until she's lonely
i'd be her friend
i'd listen to her think in silence
she'd always have access to me

i'd plan a few things
to help her escape the spaces
that drive her crazy
on those days **drifting in thought**
where she **feels less** + left
to be there for herself
i'd be there for her
my devotion **would be her potion**

curing the ache
of being wrong about people
how things end or start
i'd cover **her heart**
with mine
our two hearts would heat the cold
+ carry the load of emotion
felt after being used or disappointed
i'd hug her
wrapping my arms **around her pain**
squeezing

breathing
sending love through her veins
i just want to protect her
in all the ways

she **doesn't** need saving
she needs pursuit
and proof **that you're worthy of her time**
she's wasted plenty
gives away tons
but she's waiting for that one
that one **that transforms**
every day into magic
+ everything tragic **that happened**
ends with nights of
passionate conversation

she's patient
but **she's not waiting**
remember she doesn't need a savior

she needs **herself**
herself from you
reflecting on her, **constantly in her view**
she must **see herself** in you + **in action**
before, and not after
when she falls
if she falls
i'll catch her

place her down to rest
while i craft her wings
install them in her body so she
dares to jump for any dream
knowing **she can't fall** or fail

i'll watch as she climbs higher
the tallest of cliffs
standing in the clear
fully embracing **the space**
of being worth it

thoughts + pieces

for everything right
everything imperfect

happy + **free of second-guessing**
completely cured of fear
through this intimate projection
of being in sight + seer
i'd be her
and **her protection**

letting go
feels like

a stare-off between you + what hurt you.
your commitment to release it is not blinking.
every moment that passes triggers an eye twitch
+ you'd much rather be looking at something else
or devising a scheme to vindicate yourself, but
there's nothing left to say. it wouldn't change
things anyway. **continuing to stare, your eyes**
gloss over, fixated, noting everything you see
until all that's left is a mirror.

RUMI RYAN

@iamrumiryan
www.rumiryan.com

thank you for
sharing in this
experience
with me

-rumi